Baby Penguins at the Zoo

Cecelia H. Brannon

Enslow Publishing
101 W. 23rd Street
Suite 240
New York, NY 10011
USA

enslow.com

Published in 2016 by Enslow Publishing, LLC.
101 W. 23rd Street, Suite 240, New York, NY 10011

Library of Congress Cataloging-in-Publication Data

Brannon, Cecelia H.
  Baby penguins at the zoo / by Cecelia H. Brannon.
    p. cm. — (All about baby zoo animals)
  Includes bibliographical references and index.
  ISBN 978-0-7660-7152-0 (library binding)
  ISBN 978-0-7660-7150-6 (pbk.)
  ISBN 978-0-7660-7151-3 (6-pack)
  1. Penguins — Infancy — Juvenile literature. 2. Zoo animals — Juvenile literature. I. Brannon, Cecelia H. II. Title.
  QL696.S473 B73 2016
  598.47'139—d23

To Our Readers: We have done our best to make sure all website addresses in this book were active and appropriate when we went to press. However, the author and the publisher have no control over and assume no liability for the material available on those websites or on any websites they may link to. Any comments or suggestions can be sent by e-mail to customerservice@enslow.com.

Photos Credits: Cover, gary yim/Shutterstock.com; p. 1 leospek/Shutterstock.com; pp. 4–5 the808/ Shutterstock.com; p. 6 © iStockphoto.com/belizar73; pp. 3 (left), 8 Gridnev/Shutterstock.com; p. 10 gary yim/Shutterstock.com; pp. 12, 16 Lisa Maree Williams/Getty Images News/Getty Images; pp. 3 (right), 14 Wolfgang Kaehler/LightRocket/GettyImages; p. 18 Scott Leman/Shutterstock.com; pp. 3 (center), 20 Knumina Studios/Shutterstock.com; p. 22 The Washington Post/Getty Images.

Contents

Words to Know

chick   down   waddle

4

Who lives at the zoo?

A baby penguin lives at the zoo!

A baby penguin is called a chick.

A penguin chick has soft, fuzzy feathers called down. They are usually gray and white. But some kinds of penguins are brown.

A penguin chick cannot fly. Instead, they use their wings to swim.

A penguin chick walks funny because of its flat feet and short legs. Its funny walk is called a waddle.

A penguin chick lives with its family at the zoo. A group of penguins is called a colony.

A penguin chick eats fish, crabs, and squid. It gets food from the zookeeper.

A penguin chick makes different sounds. It chirps, squawks, and yells.

You can see a penguin chick at the zoo!

Read More

Esbaum, Jill. *Explore My World: Penguins*. Washington, DC: National Geographic Society, 2014

Ward, Finn. *Penguins at the Zoo*. New York: Gareth Stevens, 2015.

Websites

San Diego Zoo Kids: African Penguin
kids.sandiegozoo.org/animals/birds/african-penguin

SeaWorld Kids: Penguin Fact Sheet
seaworldkids.com/en/gennature/extras/animalinfo/penguin-fact-sheet/

Index

Guided Reading Level: D
Guided Reading Leveling System is based on the guidelines recommended by Fountas and Pinnell.

Word Count: 125